DISCOVER the WORLD of SQUIRRELS

©2015 HieroGraphics Books LLC
All Rights Reserved
No Unauthorized Copying,
Editing or Distribution

Photographic Images by Julia L. Wright ©2015
Cover Design by Julia L. Wright ©2015

Terms of Use and Disclaimer:
　No part of this book may be reproduced in whole or in part, or stored in a retrieval system or transmitted in any form or by any means electronic, recording, mechanical, photocopying or otherwise, without written permission of the publisher, except in the case of brief quotations embodied in critical articles or reviews.
　The Author and Publisher has strived to be as accurate and complete as possible in the creation of this book, notwithstanding the fact that due to due to the rapidly changing nature of the climate conditions and information she does not warrant or represent at any time that the all the contents within are still accurate. While all attempts have been made to verify information provided in this publication, the Author and Publisher assume no responsibility of liability for errors, omissions, or contrary interpretation of the subject matter herein.
　The information presented in this book represents the view of the author as of the date of publication, the author reserves the right to alter and update opinions and information based upon new conditions and research. We have relied on our own experience as well as many different sources for this book, and we have done our best to check facts and to give credit where it is due. In the event that any material is incorrect or has been used without proper permission, please contact us so that the oversight can be immediately corrected.
　This book is presented for informational purposes only.

For information regarding permission, write to:
info@hierographicsbooksllc.com
Manitou Springs, CO

Printed in the United States of America
First Printing, April 2015

ISBN-13: 978-1512255331
6ISBN-10: 1512255335

DISCOVER the WORLD of SQUIRRELS

Illustrated Kids Book With Fun Facts About Squirrels And Builds Kids Vocabulary

Violet Burbach

HieroGraphics Books LLC

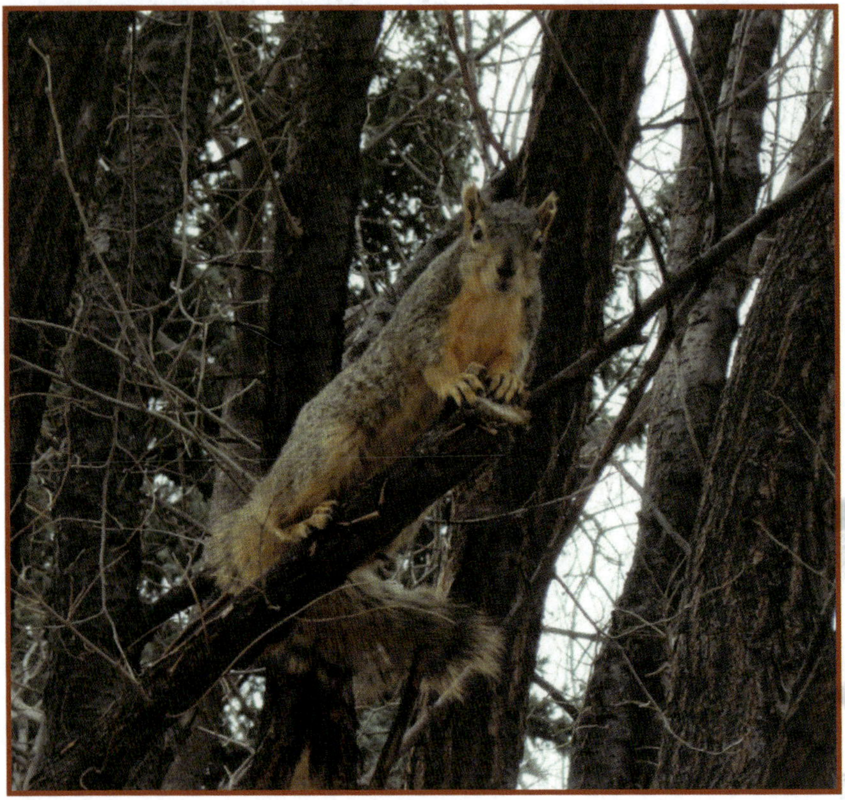

Table of Contents

Table of Contents 1
Introduction to "Discover the World of Squirrels" 3
Welcome to the World of Squirrels 5
Fox Squirrel 26
Red Squirrel 32
Eastern Gray Squirrel 34
Western Gray Squirrel 36
Black Squirrel 38
Flying Squirrel 40
Abert's Squirrel 42
Glossary 46

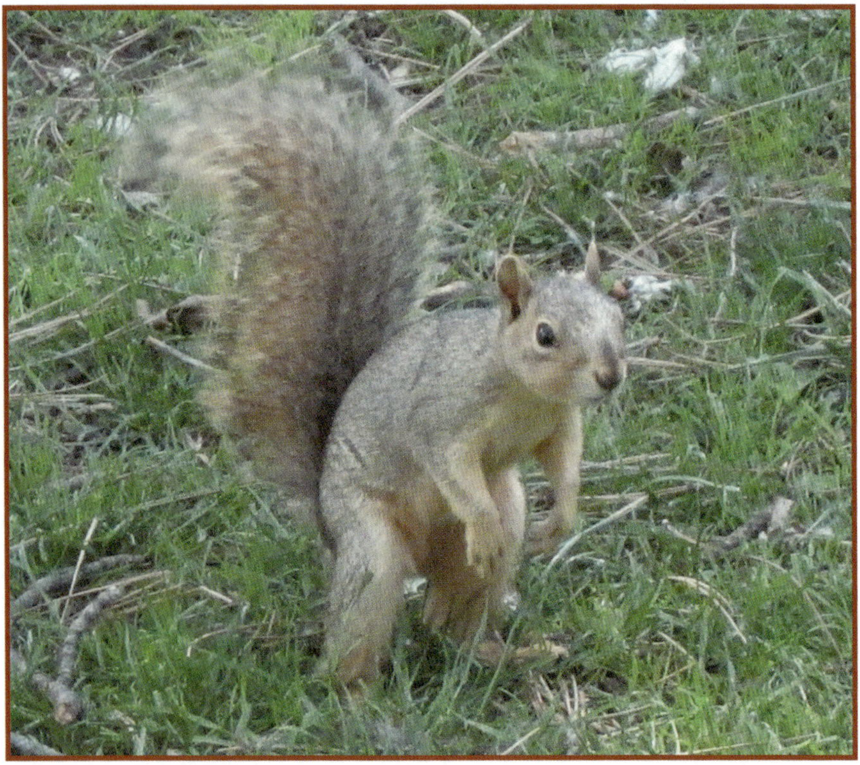

Introduction to "Discover the World of Squirrels

Some of my earliest childhood memories involve watching squirrels play in our wooded yard in northern Illinois. There were many trees that produced acorns and hickory nuts for them to eat and stash for the winter.

We often spent long stretches of time watching them scamper across the lawn or leap from a branch of one tree to land on a tiny branch many feet away in another tree. Sometimes they would sit on the windowsill and tease our little red foxy-looking dog that would go crazy barking on the other side of the glass.

And as I grew up, I never tired of watching squirrels at play.

This book is focused on presenting information about tree squirrels that live all over the world in every type of habitat.

Ground squirrels are very diverse members of the squirrel family. They bodies vary in shape and they interact with each other in very different ways than tree squirrels do. Some can live in areas where tree squirrels don't exist. Perhaps in the near future another book will come about to discover more information about ground squirrels.

The book has a glossary of words that children reading this book may not be familiar with in their current vocabulary. The first time a word in the glossary appears, it will be brown in color.

A little bonus booklet that has word search and crossword puzzles using the words in the glossary can be accessed at:

www.hierographicsbooksllc.com/squirrels-bonus/

This booklet also includes a few squirrel poems with simple illustrations and a squirrelly maze.

All of the photographs in this book that are not accredited to someone else were taken by Julia L. Wright in Colorado. We hope these images will put a smile on all our readers' faces, both young and old.

Wishing you and your kids a very enjoyable time spent learning some new words and interesting facts about these adorable furry creatures that inhabit almost every country around the world.

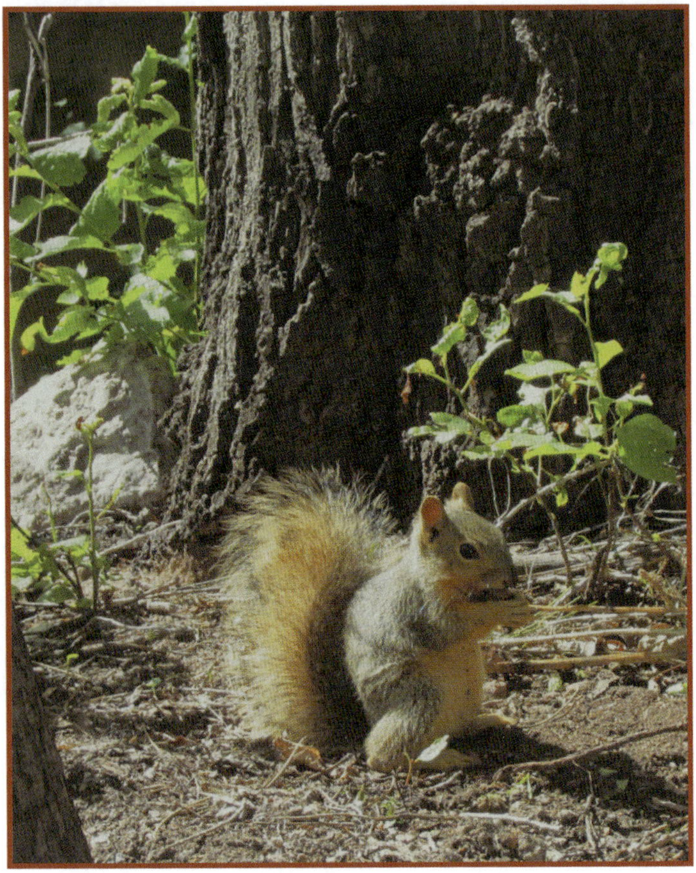

Welcome to the World of Squirrels

What is your most favorite wild animal to watch playing?

Mine is the squirrel.

   I think most children will agree that squirrels are one of the cutest wild animals living on this planet.

Do squirrels ever distract you?

Almost everyone, young and old, enjoys watching their playful antics on the ground and posing in trees.

Squirrels can be very irresistible to watch when ones sees them scampering across a lawn.

Who can resist watching their amusing aerial acrobatics?

We all enjoy watching them easily scamper up tree trunks and balance on small branches above our heads.

Many people find themselves holding their breaths when watching a squirrel doing one of its daredevil jumps from one tiny branch to another high above the ground.

Squirrels have been around for a long, long time. Fossils of squirrels date back to about 35-40 million years ago. The oldest fossils look very similar to flying squirrels.

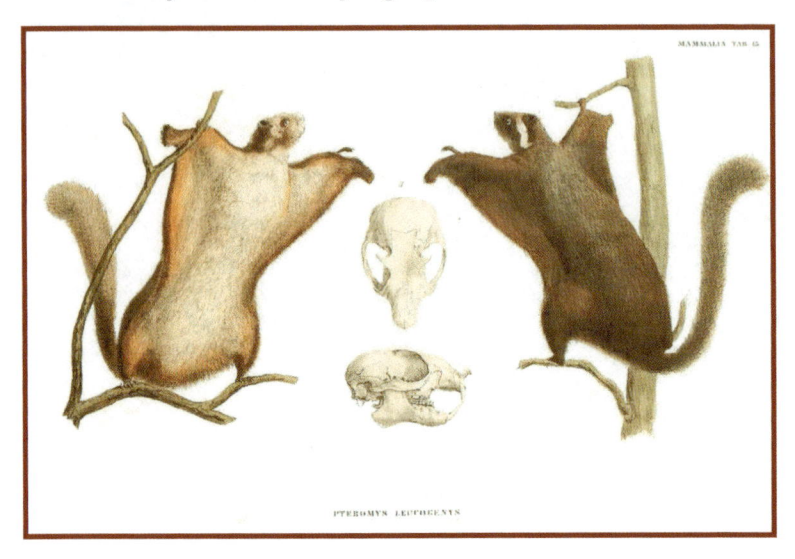

The largest distribution of tree squirrels are found in North America. It is believed that the common ancestor of all squirrels lived in North America.

Squirrels that are related to this North American subfamily are also found in Eurasia and Africa. A few species of squirrels can be found in tropical settings in Asia and South America.

Wikipedia contributor Connorma

The genus, Sciurus, is derived from two Greek words, *"skia"*, meaning shadow, and *"oura"*, meaning tail. This name alludes to the squirrel sitting in the shadow of its tail.

Wikipedia contributor Phil_PA_J.arnold.x

The squirrel family includes many different types of squirrels. There are five subfamilies of living squirrels with 285 species. It includes tree squirrels, ground squirrels, flying squirrels, chipmunks, marmots, woodchucks and prairie dogs.

Chipmunk in Bandelier National Park

Squirrels can be found all over the planet in North and South America, Africa, Europe, Asia and Australia. They can be found living in almost every type of environment except the most northern Polar Regions or extremely dry deserts. Some species of squirrels live in tropical rainforest, many live in wooded areas and a few species thrive in semi-arid deserts.

Wikipedia Contributor Sebastian Wallroth

Squirrels come in many colors that can vary even within their own species. North America has many types of squirrels.

Most squirrels are a reddish brown in color, but some have gray or even black fur.

The largest subfamily of squirrels is mainly the ground-living forms, which includes the large marmots and the popular prairie dogs. They tend to live together in communities and are much more gregarious than tree squirrels. Tree-dwelling squirrels tend to be more solitary than their ground-dwelling cousins.

Both types of squirrels typically are seen during the daytime hours, except most flying squirrels tend to be seen at night.

Marmot by Andrea Schafthuizen

Many children are familiar with squirrels because they have seen them climbing trees in their yards or when walking in parks or forested areas.

Every type of squirrel has rather large eyes, which gives them an excellent sense of vision. This is especially helpful for the tree-dwelling species.

Squirrels are very clever and can jump long distances. Some can jump between branches as far apart as two to three feet.

Wikipedia contributor Ed Sweeney

This makes it difficult for people to use bird feeders and keep the squirrels out and is the main reason some people get very frustrated with squirrels in their yards.

Squirrels rely on their claws to help them when climbing trees.

Left: Wiki Contributor Perlick Laura (grey)
Right: Wiki contributor Joe In Queens from Queens (eastern gray)

A squirrel's hind legs are longer than their front legs. This is a very unusual trait that is rarely seen in other mammals.

Most mammals can only climb down a tree hind legs first.

Tree squirrels have the unique ability of being able to descend down a tree headfirst.

People think that hanging a bird feeder off a long rope or a chain that sways in the air will keep squirrels away.

This rarely works.

A Squirrel can rotate its hind feet to allow it to reach far from a trunk, which is another way it can raid bird feeders.

(Short Story: We have tried many "squirrel-proof" bird feeders. None have actually worked very well. The best solution was placing a large metal plate on top of a very slick old metal chimney. But the clever squirrels soon learned how to jump from any car parked near it or from a nearby tree. Finding a place for it to be far enough away from anything a squirrel could climb seemed impossible in our yard.)

Squirrels have very sturdy and versatile claws they use for grasping tiny seeds and larger nuts.

They have large, very sharp gnawing incisors at the front of their mouths and flatter, grinding teeth set farther back in their mouths.

Most squirrels live on a food diet that includes all types of seeds, nuts, conifer (pine) cones, fruits, fungi, mushrooms, and green vegetation.

The early spring is the most difficult time of year for squirrels when buried nuts begin to sprout because they cannot digest them. This is the time of year when you see squirrels munching on tree buds.

Almost all squirrels are scatter-hoarders. They hoard food in numerous small caches for later recovery. Some caches are temporary, especially when created near the site when a sudden abundance of food is discovered. These are often moved within hours or a few days for reburial at a more secure area.

Many caches are more permanent and may not be retrieved until months later. Squirrels have very accurate spatial memory that makes it possible for them to remember the locations of these storage spaces. They can use various types of landmarks to relocate their caches to retrieve stored food.

A squirrel will only rely on smell when it is within a few inches of the storage location.

Squirrels are very clever and may use deceptive actions to keep other animals from stealing their stored food. A squirrel may act as if it is burying a bit of food if it thinks it is being watched.

It will prepare the spot as usual by digging a hole or widening a crack. Then it will act as if it is placing the food there while concealing the food in its mouth.

Next it will cover up the storage area as if it had placed the food inside. Such a complex series of steps and behavior suggests that squirrels are able to think about these types of things more than many other wild creatures.

Squirrels obtain water mostly from their food, but some species, such as Abert's squirrels, may be seen drinking at ponds or other standing water.

Squirrel nests that can be seen in trees are called dreys. Most tree squirrels build a nest in the forks of trees. They basically use dry leaves and twigs for their nests. Many will use long strands of grass to weave the nests together.

Other squirrels may live in a tree den in a hollowed out trunk or a large branch of a tree.

All squirrels like to line their dens with fur, leaves, moss, thistledown, dried grass, and/or feathers. These items can provide insulation for a den to reduce heat loss. A leafy cover to the den is usually built afterwards.

Some squirrels will build two different types of stick nests each year. The first is a large, round, covered shelter nest that is usually found in the top third of the tree that will be used during the winter and in the spring for birthing and rearing young.

During the summer they may create a second nest that would be more properly called a "sleeping platform." Both types of nests are built using sticks and twigs and are lined with leaves, moss, lichens and shredded bark. The birthing nest may also be lined with their own tail hair. Young or traveling squirrels will also "sleep rough" when weather permits. You may see one balanced spread-eagled high on a tree limb.

(Short Story: We have a few squirrel nests around our house. One is a very clever squirrel that discovered a pillow on a couch on our front porch. She has made her nest very warm and cozy by tearing the pillow open and taking bits and pieces of the stuffing up to her nest.)

Squirrels can give birth to a varying number of babies once or twice a year, depending on species. A baby squirrel is called a kit.

Squirrels have many natural enemies. Lynxes, bobcats, coyotes, foxes, wolves, weasels, great horned owls, hawks, and even the American crow hunt them.

Although an adult squirrel can live as long as five to ten years in the wild, most squirrels will die in the first year of life.

As in most other mammals, communication among squirrels involves both vocalizations and posturing. Each species has a quite varied repertoire of sounds it makes, including squeaks, low-pitched noises, chattering, and raspy, almost purring sounds.

Squirrels also communicate by flicking their tails and other physical gestures, including facial expressions. Tail flicking and certain sounds are used to warn other squirrels about predators. These sounds can often ward off a predator or let others know that a predator is leaving the area.

Squirrels can make an affectionate coo-purring sound. This sound is used as a contact sound between a mother and her kits. A male uses a similar sound when courting a female during mating season.

Depending upon where a squirrel lives, different types of communication are used.

Squirrels that live in large cities tend to rely mostly on the visual signals. Where as, in a heavily wooded area, they tend to use more vocal signals as there are fewer distracting noises and the density of branches and leaves restricts the range visual signals can be seen.

Fox Squirrel

The fox squirrel is also known as the eastern fox squirrel or Bryant's fox squirrel. It is the largest species of tree squirrel native to North America. Although quite different in size and coloration, they are often mistaken for American red squirrels or eastern gray squirrels where both species live.

Fox squirrels have one unusual trait that is not found in most other squirrels. They have several sets of very thick hairs or whiskers above and below their eyes, on their chin and nose, and on each forearm. They use these as touch receptors to get a better sense of the environment.

These squirrels range in body weight and size, but tend to be smaller in size in western states. Their coloration greatly varies in three distinct geographical areas. The upper body of most fox squirrels is brown-gray to brown-yellow with a typically brownish-orange underside.

In the Appalachians and other eastern regions they have more striking-patterns. These dark brown and black squirrels will have white bands on their faces and tails.

In some very isolated communities in the south they have uniform black coats. So you see how these squirrels can be confused with other species that live in the same areas.

Fox squirrels have a large range of natural habitats throughout the United States and into the southern prairie provinces of Canada. They are rarely seen in on the east coast or in New England or Pennsylvania. They have adapted to many types of habitats, but they are most often found in small patches of forests or in urban neighborhoods where groups of trees create a suitable environment. Their ideal habitat is small stands of large trees interspersed with agricultural land or homes with large backyards.

Eastern fox squirrels build leaf nests and tree dens. They often use two nests each year. One nest might be in a tree cavity and the other is a leaf nest they build. Eastern fox squirrels have also been known to also use deserted crow's nests.

Tree dens are preferred over leaf nests during the winter and for raising young. A very industrious eastern fox squirrel may make its own den in a hollow tree by cutting through to the interior. But it is more typical for them to use natural tree cavities or cavities created by northern flickers or red-headed woodpeckers.

Their most favorite trees are ones that produce winter-storable foods like nuts, such as oak, hickory, walnut, and pines. The squirrels are absent where two or more of these favorite trees don't grow. Eastern fox squirrels eat all types of nuts, including hickory nuts, buckeyes, acorns, hazelnuts and black walnuts. They will also eat seeds, buds and the bark of maple, willow and elm trees.

When gardens begin to ripen, they will munch on tomatoes, strawberries, plums, avocados, blackberries and various other fruit and vegetable plants to the distress of many gardeners.

They are very well known for stealing dried corn, peanuts and sunflower seeds from bird feeders.

Fox squirrels have no problem living around humans. They seem to thrive in crowded urban and suburban environments.

They are known to exploit these places for sources of food and nesting sites, including being very happy to nest in an attic when they can find an entrance just below a roof.

Red Squirrel

American red squirrels can be found all across North America from Arizona to the northern reaches of Canada.

Wikipedia contributor Dave S

Red squirrels are smaller in size than most other North American tree squirrels. They have reddish fur with a white underbelly. They have ear tufts similar to Abert's squirrels. *(See page 42.)*

They only come out in the day and tend to defend their exclusive territory very ferociously.

Wikipedia contributor Dave S

American red squirrels have a very specialized diet and tend to mostly eat the seeds of conifer cones. Though these tree squirrels may add other food items into their diets when the opportunity and necessity to do so presents itself.

Eastern Gray Squirrel

The eastern gray squirrel has predominantly gray fur with a white underside and a large bushy tail. It can also have a brownish colored fur. In Canada and the United Kingdom, it is generally referred to as the *"grey squirrel"*. It is a very prolific species that adapts well to many types of habitat.

Anonymous Wikipedia contributor

The eastern gray squirrel is native to areas in eastern and Midwestern United States and southerly portions of the Eastern Provinces of Canada. In Europe these squirrels are a concern as they have displaced some of the native squirrels there. There are also concerns that such displacement might happen in Italy and that gray squirrels might spread from Italy to other parts of mainland Europe.

Eastern gray squirrels have a high enough tolerance for humans and often are found living in the back yards of homes in residential neighborhoods, parks or in more rural farming environments. Here they raid bird feeders for corn, millet, peanuts or sunflower seeds. Gardeners have caught them eating various garden crops including tomatoes, corn, pumpkins, squash and strawberries.

Wikipedia contributor Kevin LawS

In the wild, eastern gray squirrels prefer to live in hardwood forests where oak and hickory trees abound rather than coniferous forests.

Western Gray Squirrel

The western gray squirrel, also know as the silver-gray squirrel, tends to live in trees along the western coast of the United States and Canada. It is the largest native tree squirrel living in the western coastal United States.

Wikipedia contributor Davefoc

Western gray squirrels live in forests located in areas ranging from sea level to elevations up to 6,500 feet. They prefer to spend most of their time in trees. Any time on the ground is spent foraging for food.

They are strictly diurnal, and feed mainly on seeds and nuts, particularly pine seeds and acorns. They also will eat berries, fungus and insects.

The dorsal fur is a silver gunmetal gray, with pure white on the underside.

They sport very long, white-edged bushy tails. Black flecks are often seen in their tails. They use their tails for balance when jumping between tree branches.

Their feet are larger than most other squirrels.

Their ears are rather large but without tufts. In the winter, the backs of their ears turn reddish-brown.

Naturespicsonline

Although they do not hibernate, they do become less active during the winter.

These squirrels are shy, and will generally run up a tree and give a hoarse chirping call when frightened.

Black Squirrel

Most black squirrels live in Eastern Canada, parts of Midwestern and the Northeastern United States. Black squirrels were in abundance throughout North America before Europeans arrived in the 16th century.

Wikipedia contributor Sujit Kumar

Its dark color is thought to have helped them hide in dense and shaded forests. Hunting and deforestation led to advantages for gray colored individuals who are now more predominant in its original habitats.

Individual black squirrels can exist wherever gray squirrels live. Black squirrels have much higher tolerance for cold, as they lose less heat than gray squirrels. This means they can live in areas that get much colder than the gray squirrel's habitats.

Wikipedia contributor Mockba1 19999

Beyond the areas of North America where black squirrels occur naturally, there are several places populations of black squirrels have been introduced and have thrived. They also live across the ocean in the United Kingdom.

Flying Squirrel

There are 44 species in the flying squirrels tribe of squirrels. There are two very distinct species. One species is native to North America, and the other known as the Siberian flying squirrel is native to parts of northern Europe. Recently, three new species of flying squirrel were found in the northeastern state of India.

Left: Wikipedia contributor Pratikppf   -   Right: Wikipedia contributor a. freeman

They are not capable of actual powered flight like birds or bats. They have a membrane of skin on either side of their body that can be expanded to allow it to glide between trees through the air.

By changing the positions of its front arms and back legs, it changes the tautness of the furry parachute-like membrane that stretches between its wrists and ankles. These adjustments then will vary the direction or height and speed of their flight in midair to guide it to is anticipated landing place.

It uses its fluffy tail to stabilize itself when in flight. Its tail works as an air-foil to help it brake before landing on a tree trunk.

Gliding, rather than climbing and leaping between trees conserves the squirrel's energy.

Unlike most squirrels, flying squirrels are usually nocturnal. They are not very adept at escaping birds of prey that hunt during the daytime.

Wikipedia contributor Shell Presto DiBaggio.

Flying squirrels eat a bit differently than most other squirrels. They are omnivorous, and will eat whatever types of food they can find in the environment where they dwell.

They can easily forage for food at night, as they have a very highly developed sense of smell that guides them to the best places that they can harvest fruits, nuts, fungi, and bird eggs.

Abert's Squirrel

Abert's squirrel is named after Colonel John James Abert, an American naturalist who organized the effort to map the American West during the 19th century. It is also known as the tassel-eared squirrel.

The most noticeable characteristic of an Abert's squirrel is their hair tufts on their ears. These extend up about an inch off of each ear. Eurasian Red Squirrels are the only other species of squirrels that sport ear tufts.

National park Service

Abert's squirrels are diurnal. They are early risers as they begin their daily activities for a short time before sunrise and stay active throughout the day. They prefer to return to their shelter before sunset.

The Abert's squirrel is a tree squirrel that lives exclusively in the Rocky Mountains from United States to Mexico in the cool, dry interior filled with ponderosa pine forests.

Douglas Haase

Abert's squirrels make almost exclusive use of ponderosa pines for nesting and food. Abert's squirrels also can be found where there are stands of Gambel oak, Colorado pinion, junipers, quaking aspen, and Douglas-fir, which all grow at higher altitudes. Others can be found in mixed conifer canyons in New Mexico.

Summer nests are built by female Abert's squirrels on ponderosa pine branches, in Gambel oak cavities, and sometimes in cottonwood branches. Most nests are built in the branches of the ponderosa pine by using short pine twigs and infected with dwarf mistletoe. They are roughly spherical and often have an added small platform extending beyond the round edge on one side.

Wikipedia contributor Unknown

Females tend to move the litter to a larger nest when their young are between three to six weeks old.

During the winter, pairs of Abert's squirrels will share a nest for shelter. This pairing usually consists of an adult female and one sub-adult.

Wikipedia contributor Sally King

    Severe winter weather is rarely a deterrent to their feeding activity. They do not need to store food, as all other North American squirrels need to do.

    Abert's squirrels can consume many parts of ponderosa pine trees year-round. The seeds are the most highly preferred item, but they also consume inner bark of young twigs, buds, and pollen cones. Gambel oak acorns, fleshy fungi and molted antlers may also provide substantial food for Abert's squirrels.

Glossary

adapts: to change a behavior so that it is easier to live in a particular place or situation.

air-foil: a body (as an airplane wing or propeller blade) designed to provide a desired reaction force when in motion relative to the surrounding air.

alludes: to speak of or hint at without mentioning directly.

ancestor: one from whom an individual, group, or species is descended.

caches: a place for hiding, storing, or preserving treasure or supplies.

conifer: any of an order of mostly evergreen trees and shrubs having leaves resembling needles or scales in shape and including forms (as pines) with true cones .

coniferous: of, relating to, or being a conifer or conifers.

courting: to engage in activity leading to mating; to seek the affections or favor of another.

deceptive: tending or having power to deceive; mislead; to lead in a wrong direction or into a mistaken action or belief.

density: how tightly or loosely packed an area is; the number of things or people in a certain area.

descended: to originate or come down from a source; or from an earlier time or generation.

desert: to withdraw from or leave without intent to return. deserted: abandoned; empty; no longer occupied.

displace: to remove from a usual or proper place; especially to expel or force to flee from home or natural habitat; to take the place of.

distract: to draw the attention or mind to something else; to upset or trouble in mind to the point of confusion.

diurnal: active chiefly in the daytime.

dorsal: relating to or situated near or on the back (as of an animal).

dreys: squirrel nest.

environments: the surrounding conditions or forces that influence or modify the whole complex of factors (as soil, climate, and living things) that influence the form and the ability to survive of a plant or animal or ecological community.

Eurasian: of mixed European and Asian origin.

excluded: to keep from entering; shut out; force out; expel.
exclusion: the act of leaving someone or something out.
exclusively: to the exclusion of anything else; alone.

exploit noun: a brave or daring act.
exploit verb: to make use of unfairly for one's own advantage.

facial: related to the face.

ferociously: intensely; extremely; acting in a violent or aggressive manner.

flecks: tiny spots of color.

frustrate: to prevent from carrying out a purpose; to check or defeat another's plan or prevent achievement of a goal; the causing of failure despite determined or repeated efforts.

fungi: any of a kingdom of living things (as molds, rusts, mildews, smuts, and mushrooms) that lack chlorophyll, are parasitic or live on dead or decaying organic matter, and were formerly considered plants.

genus: a category of classification in biology that ranks between the family and the species, contains related species, and is named by a capitalized noun formed in Latin .

gesture: an expressive movement of the body; moving the body in a way that conveys feeling or emotion.

gregarious: people or animals that are very social and enjoy being in crowds.

habitat: the place or type of place where a plant or animal naturally or normally lives or grows.

hibernate: spend the winter in a dormant state or sleep through the winter, or to stay indoors and not leave.

hoarse: having a rough or harsh sounding voice.

incisors: a front tooth for cutting; especially one of the cutting teeth between the canines of a mammal.

irresistible: impossible to resist.

interspersed: to set here and there among other things.

isolated: to be alone; have minimal contact with others; remote place that is far away from others.

kits: baby squirrels.

mating: to bring or come together as a couple to produce young.

membrane: a thin soft flexible sheet or layer especially of a plant or animal part (as a cell, tissue, or organ).

molt: to shed hair, feathers, outer skin, shell, or horns with the cast-off parts being replaced by a new growth.

native: born in a particular place or country; grown, produced, or having its beginning in a particular region.

nocturnal: active at night.

omnivorous: feeding on both animal and vegetable substances.

posturing: to take a particular posture; stance; pose.

predominant: greater in importance, strength, influence, or authority; prevailing.

predator: an animal that hunts a smaller or weaker animal.

primarily: for the most part; chiefly; in the first place; originally.

prolific: producing young in large numbers.

receptor: a receiver; any specialized cell or structure that responds to sensory stimuli.

repertoire: the stock of special skills, devices, techniques, etc. of a particular person, animal or particular field of endeavor.

residential: an area or part of a town where many homes exist.

solitary: growing or living alone; not forming part of a group.

spatial: of or relating to space.

specialized: to limit one's attention or energy to one lifestyle, business, subject, or study.

species: a class of things of the same kind and with the same name; a category of living things that ranks below a genus, is made up of related individuals able to produce fertile offspring, and is identified by a two-part scientific name.

spread-eagled: to stand or move with arms and legs spread wide.

sturdy: firmly built or made; strong and healthy in body.

subfamily: one of the subdivisions, of more importance than genus, into which certain families are divided; small group of animals within a species/family.

tolerance: ability to put up with something harmful or unpleasant; the ability to live with something so that its effects are experienced less strongly.

tropical: relating to the tropics; warm climate.

thistledown: the mass of seed-carrying fluffy bristles from the ripe flower head of a thistle.

tufts: a small cluster of long flexible outgrowths (as of hairs, feathers, or blades of grass) that are attached or close together at the base and free at the opposite end.

urban: relating to, typical of, or being a city.

versatile: able to change; able to do many different kinds of things.

visual: something that is seen; that is or can be seen; visible; relating to the sense of sight; done by sight only.

vocalizations: an act, process, or instance of creating vocal sounds.

Don't forget to get the fun little bonus booklet that has word searches and a crossword puzzle using the words found in this glossary.

www.hierographicsbooksllc.com/squirrels-bonus/

This booklet also includes a few squirrel poems with simple illustrations and a squirrelly maze.